G000078668

Shatter the Stars

Mishaal Omer

Text copyright © Mishaal Omer 2019
Design copyright © Billie Hastie 2019
All rights reserved.

Mishaal Omer has asserted her right under the Copyright, Designs and Patents Act 1988 to be identified as the author of this work.

No part of this book may be reprinted or reproduced or utilised in any form or by electronic, mechanical or any other means, now known or hereafter invented, including photocopying or recording, or in any information storage or retrieval system, without the permission in writing from the Publisher and Author.

First published 2019
by Rowanvale Books Ltd
The Gate
Keppoch Street
Roath
Cardiff
CF24 3JW
www.rowanvalebooks.com

A CIP catalogue record for this book is available from the British Library.
ISBN: 978-1-912655-12-0

For my family, my mentors, my muses,
and for you, for daring to dream.

Contents

Kingdom of Dreamers 8

dreams are desire so sharp, they dull the pain of daring to hope.

my heart aches for people I have never known.

but the goddess of death is not permitted to have a soul.

who does she become when there is no one to bear witness to her existence?

they say my name means torch, so let them watch me blaze.

Cracking Kingdom

Thorned Proses

Nothing is Right

Lost to Time

One Day

My Golden Key

Tempest

Too Caught Up

Centuries Lost

Darkness Within 24

Electricity and Lies

Wardrobe

The Catacombs of My Heart

My Demon

My Body's Battlefield

Mirrored

grief settles itself so deeply inside your bones,
you sometimes forget it's there.

I do not recognize the girl in the mirror anymore.

Invisible Scars

The Girl in the Corner

Strange Soon

Muffle My Cries

Masters of Night 38

Is there anything more beautiful than the sunset,
healing the world as it bleeds?

Constellations

the darkness sings to me in a way the morning
never has.

she is master of death at the price of her soul.

Mistress of Night

The Jester's Market

Stars

Blazing

Lost Souls 48

Shattered

I have broken so often, some of my pieces are lost.

Blood and Glass

Not a Soul Seems to Care

Beheaded at Dawn

Mother

her mind is breaking, and so is my heart.

Palace of Blood

Insane Clarity
Everywhere Lost
1842
Blazing Horses
Train to Nowhere

Destined and Cursed 64

his hands may be empty but full is his soul.
Bells of Hell
Alive
Bed of Petals
To Paris
their lies are a poison so sweet, I welcomed them with an open mouth.
Unbroken
Destiny's Death
Joust with Fate
this world is doomed and broken, and we're all breaking too.
waking up each day should be a blessing, not a curse.
Candlelight
More Storm than Girl
"What should I do?"
Drowning

Kingdom of Dreamers

This one's for the dreamers, the writers, the singers, the fighters: you can shatter the stars.

Somehow I had forgotten that dreams
were only shattered shards of brittle glass,
so when I threw my famished soul at them
in the desolate embrace of a little girl
weeping in front of a foggy shop window,
I cut myself open on their jagged edges,
the hunger of passion distracting me
from the crimson dripping slowly from my ribs.

—dreams are desire so sharp, they dull the pain of
daring to hope.

Would my fate be different?
the girl with earnest eyes and twitching fingers
if only I had remembered to return her grin
the toddler with swollen lips and feeble words
perhaps if I had paused for a moment to inquire
the man with apologetic steps and bleeding wrists
maybe if I had stopped to return his desolate gaze
If only, perhaps, maybe, I had silenced the thrum
of this noisy existence and extended a steady hand.
Would my fate be different?

—my heart aches for people I have never known.

She is cursed to be divine when all she wishes is:

to taste rain on her tongue but not the taint of ambrosia,

to dance on cobblestones but never veins of marble,

to spread her palms between stars without burning the night,

to abandon the monotonous perfection of heaven and alight upon the world of those destined to dream.

> *—but the goddess of death is not permitted to have a soul.*

Do her skirts flutter between skyscrapers of ink and paper?

Do her nostrils inhale bloody carnations and scents of earth?

Do her palms glisten from the corrupted agony of her thoughts?

Do her heartbeats race each other on a path to her dreams?

—who does she become when there is no one to bear witness to her existence?

Too caustic, they said, too coarse are your words,
so I swept them behind my sagging shelves.
Too garish, they whined, too harsh shines your spirit,
so I sheltered my glowing heart in my palms.
Too deafening, they scolded, too bold are your dreams,
so I crushed them inside my trembling fists.
Too bright, they said, too blinding are you,
but to them I say no longer.

—*they say my name means torch, so let them*
watch me blaze.

Cracking Kingdom

Rivers of red run through my kingdom;
once flowed waters of wealth.
Winds spread sickness, savage and swift,
once graced horizons of health.

Ballgowns age beneath old beds;
once danced, dared to desire.
Ashes arise and then drift away;
once fueled fiercest fires.

Dreams of death plague our souls;
once prospered peace and power.
Terrors of time ticking away,
calling my kingdom's last hour.

Thorned Proses

I like the proses with thorns,
the ones that claw at your heart,
prickle you with whims and woe,
tear the fabric of souls apart.

I like the proses with misshapen petals,
the ones with crooked intent,
make you wish and wonder and worry,
what that frenzied ink could have meant.

I like the proses with infinite layers,
swirling with dreams and desires,
of stories forgotten and places lost,
smells of tears, gunshots and fires.

I like the proses with thorns,
the ones that make my heart bleed.
For the proses that ache and the proses that burn
are the proses forever I'll read.

Nothing is Right

Somewhere between factories and flashing lights,
ballgowns have vanished and lost are the knights.
Drowned all the parchment in watery graves,
sailboats and mermaids sunk beneath waves.
Carriages and chariots no longer gleam,
people are never as sincere as they seem.
Poets and cafés have since ceased to blaze,
horizons are tainted by pollution's gray haze.
Somewhere between factories and flashing lights,
we've abandoned our spirit, and nothing is right.

Lost to Time

To all the dreamers, all the wishers,
reading by candlelight in bed.
To all the thinkers, all the weepers,
mourning words they never said.

To all the castles, all the ballrooms,
that lie frosty, dead, and dark.
To all the hopers, all the shooters,
whose arrows missed their mark.

To all the candles, all the flames,
burning wild but almost gone.
To all the fountains, all the stars,
that no one wishes upon.

To all the kings, all the soldiers,
who never lived through their prime.
To all the poems, all the songs,
written but lost to time.

One day, I'm going to publish a book
that a lonely girl can clutch to her chest,
and breathe in and write all over—
because I've been that girl,
the one who whispers the same
words from the same page,
over and over again,
imprinting ink on her soul,
because she feels it so deeply.
One day.

My Golden Key

Above my heart on a fraying cord
rests one golden key.
It dangles there but I know not where
the lock it fits may be.
Through my ears on slender hooks
float two perfect stars.
They twinkle and shine but I cannot divine
if their fire will leave me scars.
Around my wrist on a silver chain
lie three tiny charms.
They tinkle and sway but I cannot say
if they keep me from harm.
I do not know if the lock is lost,
or if the scars will last forever.
I do not know if the charms will break,
if all these bonds will sever.
Above my heart on a fraying cord,
rests one golden key.
It dangles there and I am searching for where
the lock it fits may be.

Tempest

I have not veins, but lightning,
not heartbeat, but thunder wild.
I have not eyes, but clouds,
whirlwind of words, all riled.

I have not tears, but cloudburst,
not voice, but woeful wind.
I have not lips, but chaos dark,
tornado of thoughts and sins.

I have not light, but drowning depths,
not body, but savage storm.
I have not life, but swirling death,
tempest of dreams, no form.

Too Caught Up

Too caught up in games are we,
too tangled in dreams and desire,
lost in a void of secret thoughts,
sparked words and fading fires.

Too used to night to savor sunshine,
too tired to count the stars,
drifting away on a wave of dead wishes,
swept away from shore too far.

Too weak our hearts from ruthless plague,
sick from worry on every breath,
too caught up in webs of bloody lies
to beg for the solace of death.

Centuries Lost

I should have been born in centuries lost,
when carriages danced on cobblestone,
folded between pages of history books,
my poetry might not have been so alone.

I should have been born in eras past,
when ballgowns and secrets would sing,
before the museums and dusty libraries,
when the bells on clock towers would ring.

I find myself yearning for centuries lost,
for gleaming thrones and inky letters,
for in the echoes of time and forgotten art,
everything seems to me far better.

Darkness Within

You'll find that once you wander too far from the light, the darkness itself begins to glow.

Electricity and Lies

Pity must spirits the plight of our world,
how into screaming screens it seeps and concedes,
this abode of despairing smiles and polluted dreams;
we no longer wish and we no longer read.

Laugh must ghosts of the past at our venomous
headlines,
how young boys in uniforms into wastelands are led,
but their defense of this world is worthless and cruel;
the pianos are silent and poetry is dead.

Tortured must be the souls of forgotten artists,
mourn deeply must they for our fading skies,
the opera houses are burnt, libraries don't rustle;
this world is nothing but electricity and lies.

Wardrobe

In my wardrobe, secrets I keep,
next to the thoughts stealing my sleep,
behind unspoken words and puddles of tears,
on top of the shoebox stuffed with my fears.

In my wardrobe festers old pain,
behind the bodies of monsters I've slain,
next to the memories I hope to forget,
of places and people I should never have met.

In my wardrobe lies locked up my life,
between the clouds of struggle and strife.
In its chambers, I have collected the globe,
and oh, I am lost, lost in my wardrobe.

The Catacombs of My Heart

I am locked in the catacombs of my heart,
and hollow-eyed ghosts bar every path,
each taunting me with soundless cries,
each broken fragments of my past.
There are ghosts for each unspoken word,
for each sentiment left unshared.
There are ghosts for each betrayal,
for each person whom I thought had cared.
There are ghosts for each mistake,
for each misdeed I have done.
There are ghosts for each insecurity,
for each battle I believed I'd won.
There are ghosts for each lie,
for each falsehood I have created.
There are ghosts for each pretense,
for each disguise I have fabricated.
I am locked in the catacombs of my heart,
and hollow-eyed ghosts bar every path.
I am trapped by their taunts.
I am haunted by my past.

My Demon

Between the folds of my heart, in a gilded cell,
lies a demon of doubt and despair
who leeches on dreams, has a taste for pure hope,
and always smirks behind my stare.

He coats my tongue with fiery mirth,
so each word burns as I speak,
and he jeers at me for dreading truth;
my demon preys on the weak.

Every night, when my thoughts grow loud,
he thrashes against his cage,
the demon between the folds of my heart
infests me with his rage.

My Body's Battleffield

The muffled beats of my heart echo
like broken cannons inside my chest.
Can you hear them, mama?

My shattered dreams drift away
on the crimson breeze of poppies and regret.
Do you taste them, papa?

My body rattles and wheezes each twilight
like metal rusting with blood.
Do you see me, brother?

I have defended this desolate land
of shell-holes and phantoms of the lost.
Do you know me, Lord?

Why is the fiercest battle between me and my own
soul?

Mirrored

Lonely girl of marble,
grieves but sheds no tears;
muffled woes and silent pleas,
prayers no one hears.

Wishful girl of ebony,
dreams but dares not hope,
for darkness crushes far too swift,
with nightmares she can cope.

Two lost tendrils of dark and light,
but alas, humanity!
When ebony peers into glass,
veins of marble shall she see.

The true hurt doesn't spring from the crumbling gravestone

or the crumpled photographs beneath the seats of the car.

What really aches is the moment of desolate devastation,

when you're humming their favorite song,

or packing old sweaters into collapsing boxes,

and somehow, for one wretched moment, you've ceased

to remember the person you could never have lived without.

—grief settles itself so deeply inside your bones, you sometimes forget it's there.

The stranger's eyes are swollen,
but puffier are her lips,
despair and doom unraveling
at her trembling fingertips.

Her frown is strangely empty,
but more lifeless are her cheeks,
the only evidence of her soul,
the rhythmic, pulsing beats.

The stranger stares straight at me,
her head cocks to one side
and frowns in sudden gloom,
as I wipe my swollen eyes.

—I do not recognize the girl in the mirror anymore.

Invisible Scars

She hides scars beneath her smiles
and torment behind her eyes,
but no one ever notices.
She writes stories of death and chaos,
fills poetry with heavy sorrow,
but no one ever notices.
She winces in pain when nobody's watching,
wipes away tears, face turned down,
but no one ever notices.
Her scars may be invisible,
but they do not ache any less.

The Girl in the Corner

She keeps her thoughts locked away
because she fears being heard.
She keeps her feelings bottled up
because she fears being broken.
She keeps her heart behind a shield
because she fears being understood.
But if she never learns to let go,
how will the world know she exists?

Strange Soon

Strange to think that soon,
my words will be forgotten,
my wishes lost to time,
strange to think that soon

My dreams will fade away,
my kingdom walls will crumble,
death decay my heart,
strange to think that soon

My chains will rust and break,
my thoughts become a void,
my blood dry in my veins,
strange to think that soon.

Strange to think that soon,
these pages will drift away,
tears shall drown the earth,
strange it will be soon.

Muffie My Cries

I am living (but a shadow of a life).

I dread each breath (lest I choke on my tears) and
fear this feeling in my throat (this whirlpool of worry
and woe) and pray one day my wounds (tempest of
torment inside) will bleed themselves enough (that
scars form over them)
and the beats of my heart become loud enough

(to muffle my cries).

Masters of Night

Seize rippling night between the palms of your hands and let it blaze through your soul.

The sunset bled crimson from its wounded sky,
enveloped the drowsy world in its sanguine embrace,
and, for a moment, if I strained my ears,
I could hear the symphony of glorious silence,
blanketing the weeping ferns and singing carnations,
but already the tendrils of night were creeping in,
and the clouds sank beneath the horizon.

—Is there anything more beautiful than the sunset,
healing the world as it bleeds?

Constellations

I've been hiding secrets in the constellations —
perhaps you can hear the whispers of the stars,
threads of temporal anguish and forgotten dreams,
drifting away on gales of midnight frost.

I've been hiding secrets in the constellations —
perhaps you can taste the hearts I lost,
puddles of tears no longer glistening,
dripping mirth and mercy from the night.

I've been hiding secrets in the constellations —
look up, darling, do you see?
For only at twilight are my thoughts ablaze
and only in darkness are my wishes free.

Perhaps it was the soft caress of midnight frost,
or the smirking constellations behind the moon,
or perhaps just the way the darkness enveloped me
in its embrace of liquid dreams and threads of destiny,
but I am no longer frightened by the night.

—the darkness sings to me in a way the morning
never has.

The universe crumples like velvet
beneath her bleeding fists,
gossamer strands of destiny,
fate freed by her forsaken touch.
Her anguish elicits shadowy tears
from all the fervent dreams
shattered by her desolate embrace,
but, alas, no one hears their cries but her.

—*she is master of death at the price of her soul.*

Mistress of Night

Around her throat is a crown of thorns;
rubies drip from every word,
but echoes only reach the stars,
her cries are never heard.

Around her feet are midnight shackles;
they blaze with every step.
Her cries of pain are lost to the night,
fading to wasted breath.

Around her heart is an obsidian cage,
stifling her pulsing beat.
The Mistress of Night is bloody words,
and two charred, crumbling feet.

The Jester's Market

Silence the chatter of portable poisons with flashing screens,

and perhaps rustling of enchanted parchment you shall hear.

It echoes beneath the cobblestones of this forsaken city,

and it's singing, it's chanting, for the dreamer that lends an ear.

Venture beyond the cracking threshold of your darkened room,

and perhaps the glowing lights of the market you shall see.

The Jester's spirit beckons forth your soul from its slumber,

and it's prancing, it's dancing, with whispered words and magic glee.

Come forth, run hither, my dearest children of the night,

let toppling stalls of blazing charms wrap you in their embrace,

but tarry not 'till the dawn, beware the horizon's sinful gaze,

in daylight all is lost, the Jester's Market gone, without a trace.

Stars

She gazes up at the swirling stars
and remembers every wish lost to the cosmos,
every night lying awake with her thoughts,
every stumble into darkness.
She gazes up at the swirling stars
and forgets every breathtaking eclipse,
every dream of ballgowns and magic,
every frosty twilight breeze.
She gazes up at the swirling stars
and sees only darkness,
but she forgets
that only by shadows
does the light shine
and only by night
do the stars twinkle.

Blazing

Stargazing on a cloudy night,
cloaked in shadow, devoid of light,
whispering slowly my dreams to the moon,
singing softly my heart's bitter tune.
Owls are mourning, trees groan in pain,
but I am not afraid of the night's cruel reign.
The night is black, but I am still gazing
because inside me, stars are blazing.

Lost Souls

*How brightly our souls shall shine
from their heavenly thrones among the stars.*

Shattered

Fibers of her existence fray with every passing
moment,
intertwined far too deeply with the shocked stupor
of choking despair and aching lungs.
Her screams of misery echo emptily through
sterile hallways of cotton sheets and tainted needles —
hospitals must have been designed to withstand
the shattering of a mother's soul,
their walls do not cave in like the chambers of her
heart,
and the tear-soaked bed does not collapse
under the weight of her intolerable torment,
an entire tapestry of fate ravaged, unraveled,
in this moment of desolate devastation,
her fingers rigid and refusing, curved over
six months' worth of whispered lullabies,
folded sheets and futures lost,
unworn mittens forsaken and blue,
the color of drowning and his lifeless skin.

Has your heart ever wriggled and crawled
between the scarred folds of your skin,
the razor of your smile ever stretched too sharply
over the bruised words and fading cries on your lips,
the darkness rippled too far beyond your pupils,
tainting the surface of every face you see?
Has your soul ever been shattered?

—*I have broken so often, some of my pieces are lost.*

Blood and Glass

In a faraway palace crafted from night,
a king drinks blood from glass.
Cold is his breath, frosty his eyes,
hewn is his heart from brass.

He bathes in tears of his fractured court,
whose bones support his throne,
and wicked is his red-stained grin,
as he sits in his palace alone.

Remembering days before his rebirth,
resurgence from the ashes of death,
trying to find traces of life,
but chilling remains his breath.

Sits solemnly that servant of Hell,
but bitterly does he reign.
In a faraway palace crafted from night,
he drinks away his pain.

Not a Soul Seems to Care

This world is despair, broken and gray,
time itself is languid, words but decay,
every sea is tainted by bloody regret
for this wretched age history will forget.
No longer do the nightingales sing,
desolation is all the dawn shall bring,
the streets are not paved with glory and love,
pollution has tainted even the skies above.
This world is cursed, wicked and gloom,
yet not a soul seems to care; we're resigned to our
doom.

Beheaded at Dawn

My mother's body was torn at twilight,
my father beheaded at dawn
by poisoned lips and frosty eyes
in whose revolution I played pawn.

My house set ablaze at dusk,
heart shattered on cobblestones,
and my tears flooded cracks in the street
that floats on a city of bones.

I swam through pockets of whispers
that surrounded me on the *rue*,
running wildly to my journey's end,
to the palace my people once knew.

Standing upon the tallest turret,
I sang the world my woeful song.
My spirit is heavy, I can't keep it steady,
I'm to be beheaded at dawn.

Mother

Sick my mother lies, blood trickling from her lips,
and yet I feel no pity as her feeble body shifts.
My mind is void and empty, my words somewhere
gone;
all I do is watch her writhe before the break of dawn,
eyes bloodshot and torn, beastly and so wild,
pleading with the ruthless world, pleading with her
child.
But in vain does my mother tremble, in vain does
she cry;
I sense a silent visitor—Death is creeping by.
He steals the breath from her broken lungs, the last
beats from her heart,
and he nods to me, silent and still, a daughter not
breaking apart.
Tears are not filling my eyes, my breath stays
steady and slow,
but I should be breaking, I should weep, mourn my
mother, I know.
Oh, how I wished I loved her, that woman so vain
and bold,
but it is too late, my mother won't wait, her body
lies there cold.

Her eyes no longer dance and swirl with stories,
her voice seems to me foreign and forlorn,
the woman I once knew was bold, bright, colorful, yet
humans are nothing more than a product of our
memories
and my grandma's memories are seeping out
through her
aching back and prosthetic knee caps,
leaving her stranded in a faded existence,
almost oblivious to her loss, yet not quite.

—her mind is breaking, and so is my heart.

Palace of Blood

In the realm of my heart, deep down inside, lies a palace coated in gold,

which in decades past was merry and wild and a thousand people could hold.

My palace always smelled of heaven, its stairways always gleamed,

and its paradise would last forever, at least to me it seemed.

But a strange wind blew through my palace that night; its walls were soaked in blood.

All the joy of my palace was lost, all the hope erased by the flood.

In the realm of my heart, deep down inside, I still keep my palace of gold,

but my palace lies dead, its walls have been bled, my palace lies dark and cold.

Insane Clarity

I seem to have misplaced my sanity,
just awoken to realize it's gone.
Perhaps the phantoms of dead poetry stole it,
or it floated away on the dawn.
I seem to have misplaced my sanity—
please check behind that folded page.
Maybe I plucked it right out of my mind
in a sudden frenzy of wicked rage.
What shall I do? My sanity's lost,
yet I'm too frightened to find it again,
for without its restraint, without its fear,
my mind's clearer than it's ever been.

Everywhere Lost

I am lost in a maze of words
with nowhere to go but deeper.
I am stranded on a mountain of thought
and the climb grows ever steeper.

Locked inside a cage of ink,
sheltering my heart in my hands,
drifting aimlessly from sea to sea,
urged on by whispered commands.

The words are speaking to me now.
I hear them crisp and clear.
I am lost in a maze of words,
alone and chained by fear.

1842

Crimson cheeks and tattered silk,
eyes too bright yet broken still,
fingers trembling, clutch with greed,
powder cursed, forsaken need,
bloody souls and glinting gold,
fractured stories never told,
hasty pleasure and mingled breath,
crooked smiles, mercy, death.

Blazing Horses

Horses leaving trails of fires,
infecting my land with funeral pyres.
Tracks of blood seeping through stone,
horses crushing piles of bones.

Horses casting fleeting shadows,
rivers of tears flooding meadows.
Horses of death, rattling chains,
horses spreading wounds and pain.

Horses stealing my country's life,
leaving behind clouds of strife.
Horses leaving trails of fires,
infesting my land with funeral pyres.

Train to Nowhere

Those who board the train to nowhere
often lose their minds,
shedding memories on cursed tracks,
passengers of time.

Unknown are their destinations,
untraveled are their paths.
The train to nowhere never ends,
wheels turning in its wrath.

The train of lost souls never halts.
Its fuel does not run low,
for it drains its passengers of life,
until the void is all they know.

Destined and Cursed

Destiny and fate, the most glorious and most beautiful of all curses.

He stretched his hands out between the folds of the
sky,
mendicant palms barren and trembling with hope,
praying perhaps for the jingle of a copper pittance,
dreaming perhaps for a single tear from the clouds.

  —his hands may be empty but full is his soul.

Bells of Hell

If what the critics crow is true, the presses preach
but right,
then Hell shall blaze fierce with poets and singers,
we'll blind the angels with our light.
If powdered wigs with faith do lie, monocles dress
the wise,
then gardens shall blossom on our crumbling graves,
and even jealous will be the skies.
If crumpled newspapers once garnered praise,
whispering history books once could sing,
we'll live on forever, eternal our souls,
let the bells of Hell now ring.

Alive

Empty sits my box of words
for my stories have been told.
Restless stirs my solemn soul
for slipping is its hold.
No more heart do I have to give,
no smiles and winks to share,
but assured beats my body's drum,
for I spread them everywhere.
In tired bliss do my eyelids close;
now begins my final dive.
I am standing at the gates of Death,
yet I feel the most alive.

Bed of Petals

Once, in a withered kingdom of old,
the princess escaped from her tower;
night was her cloak as she darted through leaves,
fled through a forest of flowers.

She halted her frenzy, planted her feet,
her breath came in heaving sighs,
but her soul was rejoicing, dancing in glee
for the first time she could see the skies.

Between folds of the forest, silent save crickets,
she discovered mysterious delight;
a bed of rose petals spread on the moss,
glowing with some unearthly light.

The princess yawned softly, eyelids drooping;
the strewn petals seemed divine.
She winked at the blossoms, tossing her hair,
and began to slowly recline.

How fierce flamed her relief for petals so soft,
did not see the thorns beneath that bloody red;
when guards traced her steps to that forest cruel,
the princess lay in her crimson deathbed.

To Paris

The Seine rippled with the crimson passion of my countrymen,

and the cobblestones floated on the tears of our empty souls,

but your dusty roses and bustling alleyways still sang to me,

and so, as I watched you burn, Paris, Paris, my darling,

and the waves of your ruination swept over the unforgiving world,

I inhaled the tang of bloody ink and crumpled parchment at your core,

and I couldn't help but smile.

They slid sweet deceit between my lips
as if it would dissolve like sticky candy
but instead it began coating my veins
with poison so saccharine and so smooth
that my heart became an endless wound
festering like a cavity against my soul.

—their lies are a poison so sweet, I welcomed
them with an open mouth.

Unbroken

There was a broken railroad track,
rusted over and almost black,
that snaked across the frosty ground
behind our camp's deathly mound.

The vindictive demons brought me in,
a new addition to their collective sin.
I did not know what horrors awaited
through the skeletal veil they had created.

Into imprisonment I was led.
Only a number, they shaved my head,
stripping me of my meager possessions,
using the power of their oppression.

I was shoved into the defeated line
in which, of hope there was no sign,
but I stood up tall and arched my back.
I wielded hope that they all lacked.

I slaved all day, deprived of pause.
Escape was a defeated cause.
My back protested and threatened to break,
but my resolve refused to shake.

There was a broken railroad track,
rusted over and almost black,
that snaked across the frosty ground
behind our camp's deathly mound.

Yet as long as I would hope,
as long as I could cope,
I would step over the fragmented track
and forever stay unbroken.

Destiny's Death

Threads of destiny weaving my woes,
spinning so softly and whispering slow,
bringing me sins and shadows and strife,
threads of fate directing my life;
they shatter my heart, with a snap, with a twist;
the pain makes me wonder if I will be missed.

Joust with Fate

Who am I to joust with fate,
that fearsome frenzied foe?
I will not last the sunset next.
Death creeps inside the snow.

Threads of destiny pulling taut,
my wounds still bleeding and raw,
tears trailing rivers of loss,
mourning places I never saw.

Death creeps in, a grisly embrace,
stealing memories from my mind,
yet who am I to joust with fate?
I couldn't stand up to time.

If you have seen young men with graying hair,
broken by the sounds of gunshots and the smell of
smoke,
or children whose bones protrude from their waxy skin
as they whimper for the mercy of early death,
if you have seen a girl curled around her two
tearing wrists
scratching to rid her own body of its soul,
or a father clutching the lifeless fingers of his child
his tears pooling with crimson on the ground,
if you have seen for yourself this shattered world,
then I suppose you already know.

—*this world is doomed and broken, and we're*
all breaking too.

Can we rewind to when the world was not so
frightening
when reading the headlines never made me afraid,
and instead of gunshots, I would dread bright
lightning?
In years past discrimination and doubt never survived,
my skin color did not make my body vulnerable,
and instead of collapsing, crashing, we thrived.
People smiled at each other and didn't wince,
but recently something in our world shattered,
nothing's quite been the same ever since.

*—waking up each day should be a blessing, not
a curse.*

Candlelight

Candle burning, candle bright,
casting shadows through the night.
It will not stay, it will not last,
my only candle burning fast.

It watches as I weave my words
into tapestries of song.
It watches, and it seems to me,
my candle sings along.

As it burns, the light grows dim
I watch it in dismay.
I see it falter, I see it flicker
I watch my candle sway.

Candle burning, candle bright
casting shadows through the night.
My candle flickers, candle sways,
I blow my candle's light away.

More Storm than Girl

Her smile is a strike of lighting,
laughter a clap of thunder,
but the calm is only a facade,
serenity before a savage storm,
and when she is unleashed,
it will be perfectly clear
why only the wildest storms
are named after people.

"What should I do?"

Breathe, breathe, until your lungs
inhale coarse corruption and exhale clarity.
Speak, speak, until your words blaze your soul
a path through the dark devastation.
Laugh, laugh, until the echoes of your jubilation
resound through abandoned valleys.
Dream, darling, dream until the very stars
shatter at your fingertips.

Drowning

Amidst the chaos and anarchy,
the stress of everyday existence,
I was drowning,
I was drowning.
Tied down by the stares of society,
the sharp glares of their judgment,
I was drowning,
I was drowning.
Crushed by the pressure of friendships,
the weight of meaningless promises,
I was drowning,
I was drowning.
Overwhelmed by the need to live,
I wrote until my lungs inhaled creativity and exhaled
clarity.
Writing is what saved me
from drowning,
from drowning.

The aching, the dreaming, the wishing:
they do not end here.
You'll leave fragments of your soul
tucked between folded pages,
nestled between old photographs,
fading into the space between memories.
The ink spilling forth from my heart,
silent it rests here, but dreams do not end,
and hope shall never die.

What is poetry but molten dreams of ink,
an author's soul bleeding its way onto paper?

Author Profile

Mishaal Omer is a dreamer. When she does not have a novel in her hands or a pen between her lips, you can find her traveling to historical monuments across the world, frequenting local bookshops, going to school, or daydreaming about the impossible. She loves to read and write poetry and fantasy, and her goal is for her words to impact her readers' lives—to leave a small mark on their soul. *Shatter the Stars* is a project born from her fascination with the stars, destiny, souls, nightmares, and—above all—words.

CPSIA information can be obtained
at www.ICGtesting.com
Printed in the USA
BVHW082240070519
547697BV00001B/159/P

9 781912 655120